I0776106

This book belongs to:

____

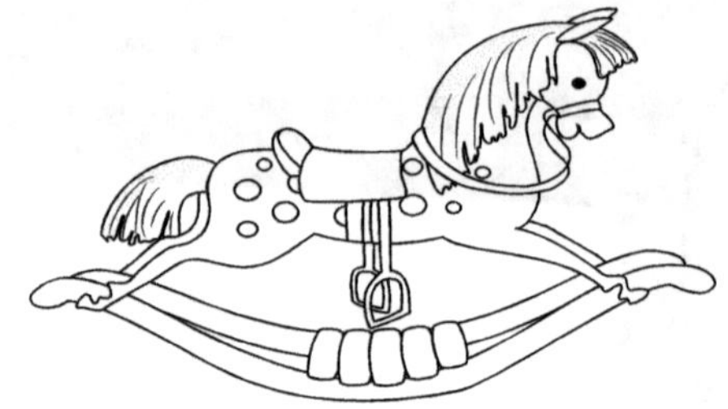

To A Very Sweet
Granddaughter!
Merry Christmas
Coloring Card

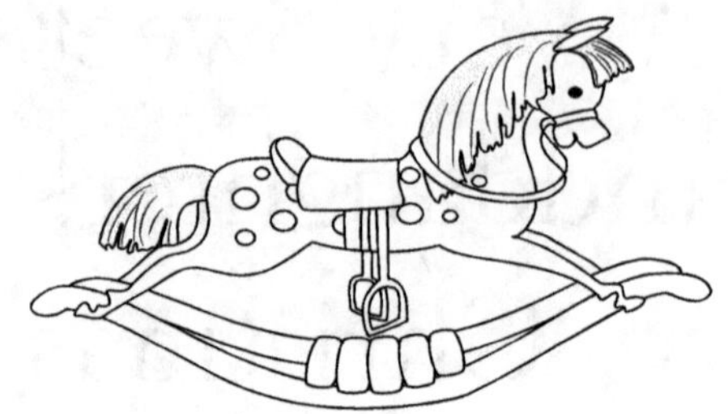

Joy to the world!

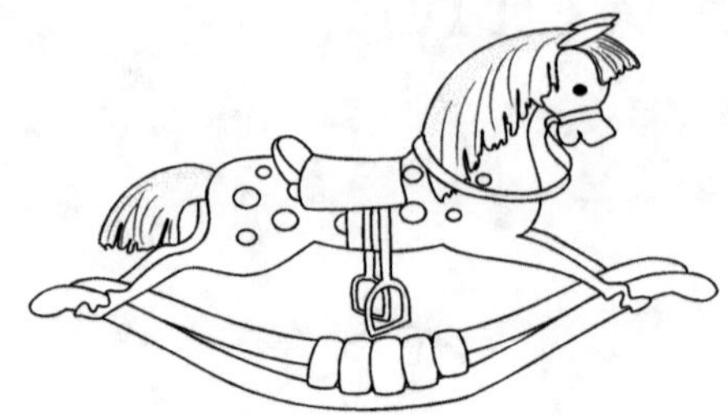

Warm wishes to you!

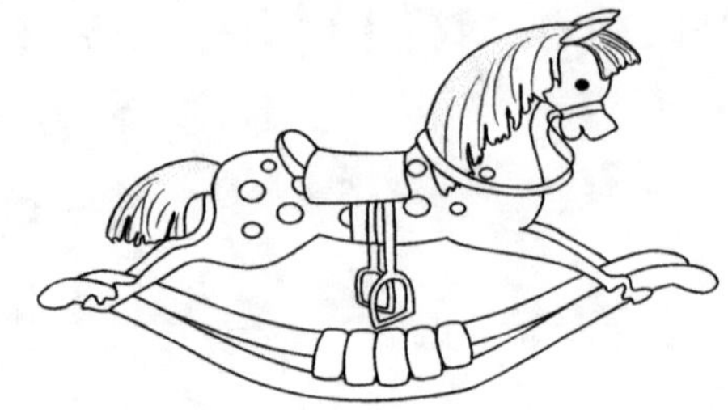

Merry and Bright!

Tis the season to be jolly,
fa la la la la la la la lamb!

It's the best Christmas ever!

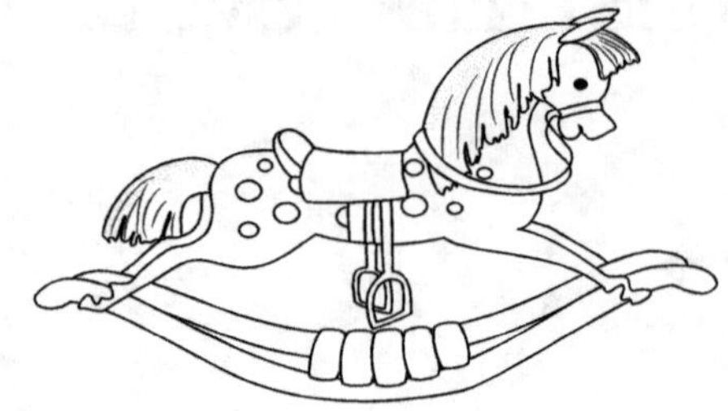

Joy to the animals!

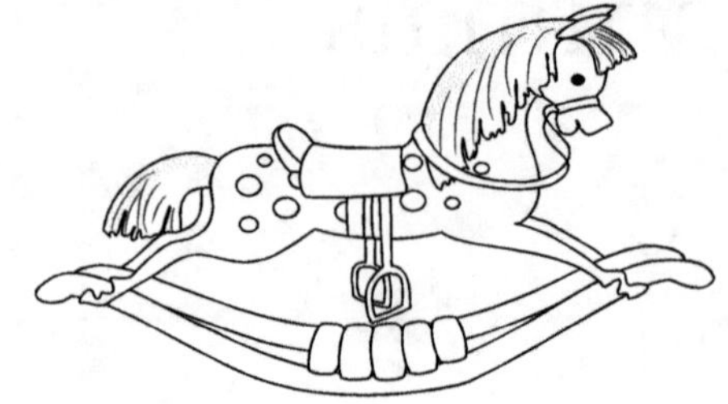

Santa's magic reindeer!

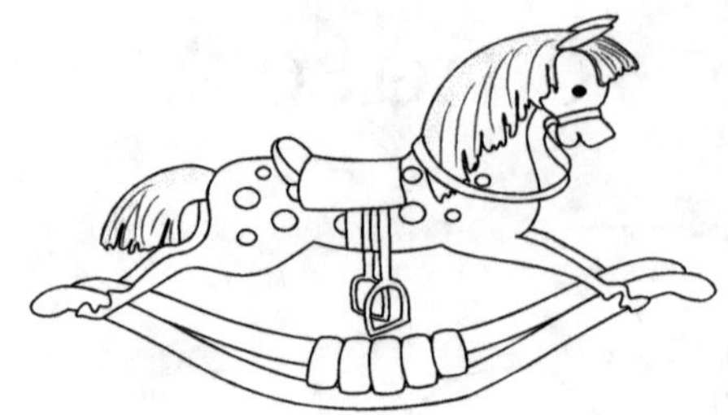

One of Santa's helpers!

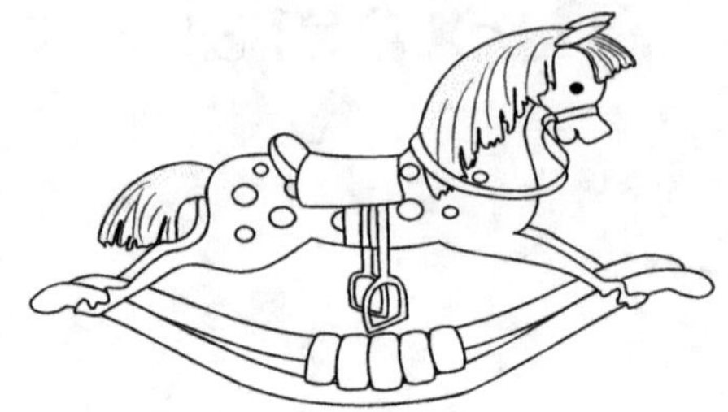

Flying in a winter wonderland!

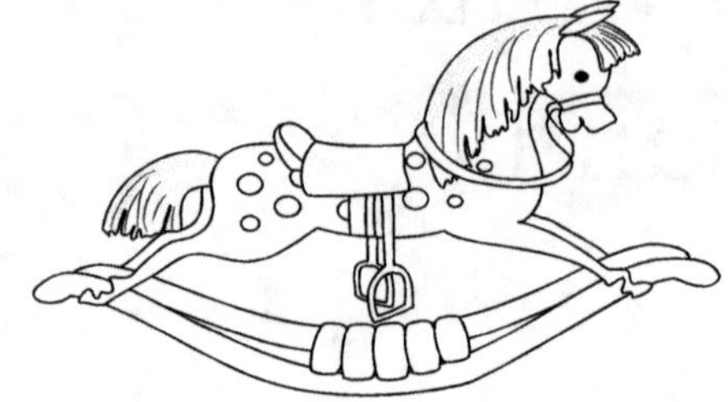

Copyright 2017
Florabella Publishing
All rights reserved. No part of this book may
be reproduced in any form or by any electronic
or mechanical means including information
storage and retrieval systems, without
permission in writing from the authors. The
only exception is by a reviewer, who may
quote short excerpts in a review.

To A Very Sweet Granddaughter!
Merry Christmas
By Florabella Publishing, LLC